KU-022-152

One, Two, Flea!

Allan Ahlberg

Colin McNaughton

One, Two, Flea!
Tiny Tim

WALKER BOOKS

LONDON

One, Two, Flea!

One, two, three,
mother finds a flea,
puts it in the teapot
to make a cup of tea.

The flea jumps out,
mother gives a shout,
in comes father
with his shirt hanging out.

Four, five, six,
father's in a fix,

wants to get the billy goat
to hatch a few chicks.

The chicks hatch out,
father gives a shout,

in comes granny
with her hair sticking out.

Seven, eight, nine,
granny's doing fine,
scrubs all the children
and pegs them on the line.

The line gives way,
granny shouts 'Hey!'
'Wow!' shout the children...

…and they all run away.

Tiny Tim

I have a little brother,
his name is Tiny Tim,
I put him in the bath-tub
to teach him how to swim.

He drinks up all the water,
he eats up all the soap,
he goes to bed
with a bubble in his throat.

In comes the doctor,
in comes the nurse,

in comes the lady
with the alligator purse.

'Dead!' says the doctor.
'Dead!' says the nurse.
'Dead!' says the lady
with the alligator purse.

But he isn't!

POP!

I have a little sister,
her name is Lorelei,
I push her up the chimney
to teach her how to fly.

She runs about the roof-tops,
she chases all the crows,
she goes to bed
with a feather up her nose.

In comes the doctor,
in comes the nurse,

in comes the lady
with the alligator purse.

'Dead!' says the doctor.
'Dead!' says the nurse.
'Dead!' says the lady
with the alligator purse.

But she isn't!

The End

KT-162-020

All children have
a great ambition to read
to themselves...

and a sense of achievement when they can do so.
The **read it yourself** *series has been devised to*
satisfy their ambition. Since many children learn
from the Ladybird Key Words Reading Scheme,
these stories have been based to a large extent
on the Key Words List, and the tales chosen are
those with which children are likely to be familiar.

The series can of course be used as supplementary
reading for any reading scheme.
Wizard of Oz is intended for children reading up to
Book 4c of the Ladybird Reading Scheme. The
following words are additional to the vocabulary
used at that level –

Dorothy, cyclone, picks, takes, strange,
land, witch, killing, wicked, asks, didn't,
shoes, magic, them, Emerald, city, Oz,
wizard, soon, scarecrow, where, brains,
tin, woodman, heart, lion, courage,
green, spectacles, more, sadly, sends,
monkeys, throws, drops, melts, goodbye

A list of other titles at the same level will be
found on the back cover.

Published by Ladybird Books Ltd Loughborough Leicestershire UK
Ladybird Books Inc Lewiston Maine 04240 USA

© LADYBIRD BOOKS LTD MCMLXXX
All rights reserved. No part of this publication may be reproduced, stored in a retrieval
system, or transmitted in any form or by any means, electronic, mechanical, photo-copying,
recording or otherwise, without the prior consent of the copyright owner.

Printed in England

Wizard of Oz

adapted by Fran Hunia
from the original story by L F Baum
illustrated by Brian Price Thomas

Ladybird Books

Dorothy is at home on the farm
playing with her little dog.
She sees a cyclone coming.
She picks up her little dog
and takes him into the house.

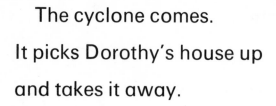

The cyclone comes.
It picks Dorothy's house up
and takes it away.

The house comes down
in a strange land.
A good witch comes to see Dorothy.
She thanks Dorothy
for killing the wicked witch.

"What wicked witch?"
asks Dorothy.
"I didn't kill a witch!"

"Yes, you did,"
says the good witch. "Look."

Dorothy looks down
and sees that her house
has landed on the wicked witch.
Dorothy can see
the witch's shoes.

The good witch
picks up the shoes
and gives them to Dorothy.

"Here you are," she says.

"You can have

the wicked witch's shoes.

They are magic."

Dorothy thanks the good witch
and puts the shoes on.

"I want to go home,"
says Dorothy.
"Can you help me, please?"

"You will have to go
to the Emerald City and ask Oz,"
says the good witch.
"Oz is a wizard. He will help you."

Dorothy and her little dog
go off to look
for the Emerald City.
Soon they see a scarecrow.

"Where are you going?"
asks the scarecrow.

"We are going
to the Emerald City to see Oz,"
says Dorothy.

"Can I go with you?"
asks the scarecrow.
"I want to ask Oz
to give me some brains."

"Come on, then," says Dorothy.

Dorothy, her dog,
and the scarecrow go on.
Soon they see a tin woodman.

"Where are you going?"
asks the tin woodman.

"We are going
to the Emerald City to see Oz,"
says Dorothy.

"Can I go with you?"
asks the tin woodman.
"I want to ask Oz
to give me a heart."

"Come on, then," says Dorothy.

They all go on.

Soon they see a lion.

"Where are you going?"
asks the lion.

"We are going
to the Emerald City
to see Oz," says Dorothy.

"Can I go with you?"
asks the lion.
"I want to ask Oz
to give me some courage."

"Come on, then," says Dorothy.

They all go on.
Soon they come
to the Emerald City.
A man gives them
some green spectacles.
They put the spectacles on
and go into the city.
It is all green.

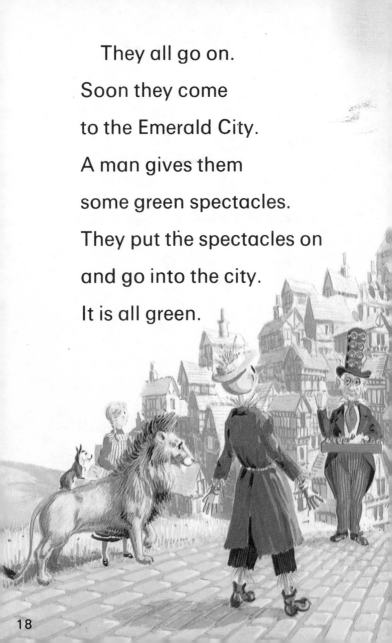

A green girl takes Dorothy
to see Oz.
Oz looks at Dorothy's shoes.

"Where did you get
the magic shoes?" he asks.

"My house landed
on the wicked witch
and killed her," says Dorothy.

"I see," says the wizard.
"And what do you want me for?"

"I want to go home,"
says Dorothy.
"Can you help me, please?"

"You can do something for me, and then I will help you," says Oz.

"What do you want me to do?" asks Dorothy.

"There is one more wicked witch in this land," says Oz. "I want you to kill her."

"I can't do that," says Dorothy.

"You have to," says the wizard, "or I will not help you."

Dorothy goes sadly away.

The scarecrow goes to see Oz.

"Please can you give me
some brains?" he asks.

"You will have to do
something for me," says Oz.
"Then I will give you some brains."

"What do you want me to do?"
asks the scarecrow.

"Kill the wicked witch," says Oz.

The scarecrow goes sadly away.

The tin woodman
goes to see Oz.

"Please can you give me a heart?"
he asks.

"You will have to do
something for me," says Oz.
"Then I will give you a heart."

"What do you want me to do?"
asks the tin woodman.

"Kill the wicked witch," says Oz.

The tin woodman
goes sadly away.

The lion goes to see Oz.

"Please can you give me some courage?" he asks.

"You will have to do something for me," says Oz.
"Then I will give you some courage."

"What do you want me to do?" asks the lion.

"Kill the wicked witch," says Oz.

The lion goes sadly away.

"We will have to kill
the wicked witch,
or Oz will not help us,"
says the scarecrow.

They all go off

to look for the wicked witch.

The wicked witch sees them coming.

She sends some magic monkeys

to get Dorothy.

The magic monkeys

take Dorothy to see the witch.

The witch sees

Dorothy's magic shoes.

She wants them.

"Give me the magic shoes,"
she says.

"No," says Dorothy.
"They are my shoes."

The wicked witch makes Dorothy
work for her.
She wants Dorothy
to take her shoes off
so that she can take them.

Dorothy is working

in the witch's house.

The witch gets

one of her magic shoes.

Dorothy has some water.

She throws it at the witch,

and the witch drops the shoe

and melts away.

Dorothy goes to look
for the scarecrow,
the tin woodman,
and the lion.

"I have killed the witch,"
she says.
"We can go and see Oz,
and he will give us
all the things we want."

They all go to the Emerald City.
The scarecrow goes to see Oz.

"We have killed the wicked witch,"
he says.

Oz makes some brains

and gives them to the scarecrow.

He gives the tin woodman a heart

and the lion some courage.

They are all pleased.

Dorothy goes to see Oz.

"Please send me home,"
she says.

"I can't send you home,"
says Oz sadly.
"I am not a wizard at all.
I can't do magic."

"What can I do?" asks Dorothy.
"I want to go home."

"There is one more good witch
in this land," says Oz.
"Go and see her.
She will help you."

43

Dorothy, her dog, the scarecrow,
the tin woodman, and the lion
all go off to see the good witch.

"What can I do for you?"

asks the good witch.

"I want to go home,"

says Dorothy.

"Can you help me, please?"

The good witch looks
at Dorothy's shoes.

"You have magic shoes,"
she says.
"They will take you home.
All you have to do is ask them."

48

Dorothy thanks the good witch.

She says goodbye

to the scarecrow,

the tin woodman, and the lion.

Then she picks up her little dog.

"Magic shoes,
please take me home,"
she says,
and soon she is at home
on the farm.